MINDFULNESS
FOR
every
day

YVETTE JANE

summersdale

MINDFULNESS FOR EVERY DAY

Copyright © Summersdale Publishers Ltd, 2016

Research by Yvette Jane

Design by Luci Ward

Illustrations © Shutterstock.com

Summersdale Publishers Ltd
46 West Street
Chichester
West Sussex
PO19 1RP
UK

www.summersdale.com

Printed and bound in India

ISBN: 978-1-78685-556-5

Substantial discounts on bulk quantities of Summersdale books are available to corporations, professional associations and other organisations. For details contact general enquiries: telephone: +44 (0) 1243 771107 or email: enquiries@summersdale.com.

INTRODUCTION

In a busy and hectic world, we could all benefit from slowing down and creating some peace, space and calm for ourselves.

Truly reaching a state of calm might seem unattainable, but with practice it is possible and the impact it can have on your life is immeasurable. A certain amount of pressure can be good for us. It can drive us to take action and feel more energised. If left unchecked, however, pressure can escalate and affect every part of our life, from our diet, to our social life, and how well we sleep at night.

Whether you encounter stress at work or at home, the easy-to-follow tips in this book will help you to free your mind of worries and handle the strains of life with greater ease. There is no quick fix, but these tips will start you on the path to a new, calmer outlook.

Nature does not hurry, yet everything is accomplished.

Lao Tzu

We all dash from one place to another – slow down with mindful walking. Take slower breaths, watch your feet as you place them on the ground, and bring awareness to your body as it moves.

Many of us go through daily routines barely noticing what we have just done, and functioning on automatic pilot. Sometimes even the simplest tasks can be done in a mindful way, so that we are totally aware of the present moment. For instance, make your bed each morning purposefully so you create a calm transition from bedroom and sleep to the outside world and the rest of your day. When cleaning your teeth, be curious and alert about yourself, noticing every sensory detail, and find a few minutes in your morning routine to sit quietly and contemplate the day ahead, instead of rushing straight into your day's activities.

DO not MISS YOUR APPOINTMENT WITH LIFE.

When you're out and about, whether it's in a vehicle or on foot, pause to appreciate your surroundings, really seeing the things you take for granted every day. You'll be surprised at how much you missed before!

THERE IS
JOY
IN JUST BEING.

If you have pain or tension in a part of your body today, focus on the place of discomfort and imagine a warm light clearing the pain away, leaving you relaxed and breathing steadily.

As you prepare a meal, stop to notice every culinary aroma and allow each aroma to awaken your sense of smell. Before every meal, take a moment to quietly give thanks for the food you are about to eat. Focus all your attention on eating, rather than anything else going on around you – try mealtimes without the TV on in the background and see if it makes you appreciate the food and the feeling of being full more than usual. It also helps to place your fork down in between mouthfuls, savouring each mouthful and chewing slowly to bring awareness to every taste sensation.

Everything is phenomenal; everything is incredible; never treat life casually.

Abraham Joshua Heschel

Find a few minutes every morning to sit in silence and greet the day ahead, instead of rushing into your day's activities, and again at the end of each day try to find a calm, silent space to wind down and relax before bedtime.

True solitude
is a din of
birdsong,

seething leaves,
whirling colours,
or a clamour of
tracks in the snow.

Edward Hoagland

Positivity is key to a mindful existence. Decide that from now on you will stop spreading bad news and only share good! If you find yourself dwelling on something negative, bring to mind a beautiful image and allow yourself to be soothed, to help turn your thoughts towards the positive. Read something positive before you go to sleep at bedtime, and repeat this affirmation to yourself at regular intervals: 'My thoughts are filled with positivity and my life is plentiful with prosperity.'

LIFE IS LIVED TODAY NOT TOMORROW

Place a photograph of nature, someone special or something that makes you smile in a place where you spend much of your time, such as next to your computer screen or as your screen saver. Look at it often and allow yourself to relax.

The Sanskrit greeting, *namaste*, can be interpreted as 'the light in me greets the light in you'. Step back and fully see the people you know for who they are, not for what they do or what they look like.

KNOWLEDGE IS LEARNING SOMETHING EVERY DAY.

WISDOM IS LETTING GO OF SOMETHING EVERY DAY.

Zen proverb

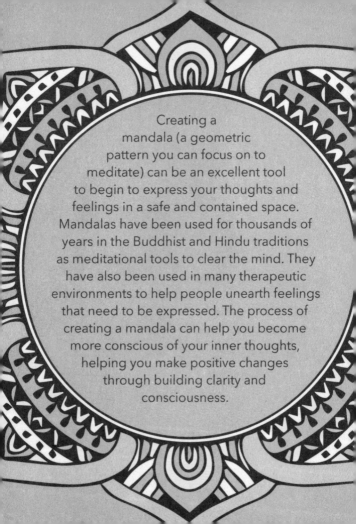

Creating a mandala (a geometric pattern you can focus on to meditate) can be an excellent tool to begin to express your thoughts and feelings in a safe and contained space. Mandalas have been used for thousands of years in the Buddhist and Hindu traditions as meditational tools to clear the mind. They have also been used in many therapeutic environments to help people unearth feelings that need to be expressed. The process of creating a mandala can help you become more conscious of your inner thoughts, helping you make positive changes through building clarity and consciousness.

You can find out more about mandalas from a good reference book, or you can create your own. There are plenty of popular mindfulness colouring books available for adults containing beautiful mandalas to colour in and help you relax.

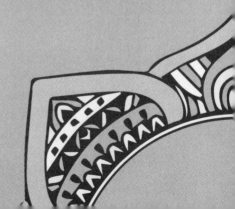

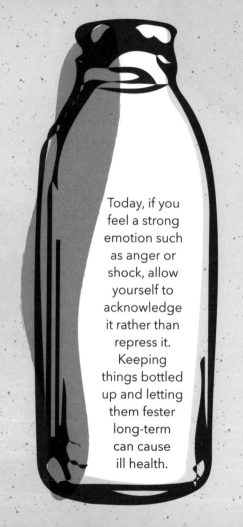

Today, if you feel a strong emotion such as anger or shock, allow yourself to acknowledge it rather than repress it. Keeping things bottled up and letting them fester long-term can cause ill health.

INSTRUCTION FOR LIFE:

pay attention.

Do you have the patience to wait till your mud settles and the water is clear?

Can you remain unmoving till the right action arises by itself?

Lao Tzu

Do you remember the last time you had an uncontrollable fit of giggles? Relive the memory and laugh yourself silly again. If something amuses you, let the laugh escape out loud: not only is it a great release, it has some other amazing benefits too. A good old belly laugh can also help lower blood pressure, tone those abs, reduce stress hormone levels, improve cardiac health, trigger natural painkillers and feel-good chemicals (endorphins) and generally make you feel much better. Join a laughter club or go with friends to see some stand-up comedy. Sometimes we need to lighten up!

Haha

Haha

Haha

Haha

NEVER BE AFRAID TO SIT AWHILE AND THINK.

Lorraine Hansberry

Have a mindful weekend without clocks or watches. Listen to your body instead – you choose when to get up, when to eat, what tasks you feel like doing and the length of time you spend on them.

NOTICE BIRDS – FLYING OUTSIDE
YOUR WINDOW, PADDLING ON A
POND, CHATTERING IN THE SHRUBS
OR FEEDING ON THE GROUND.
WILDLIFE CAN MAKE YOU SMILE AND
INSPIRE YOUR SENSE OF WONDER.

The moment you accept yourself just as you are is the moment you find peace.

Joy is everywhere;

It is in the earth's green
covering of grass;

In the blue serenity
of the sky.

Rabindranath Tagore

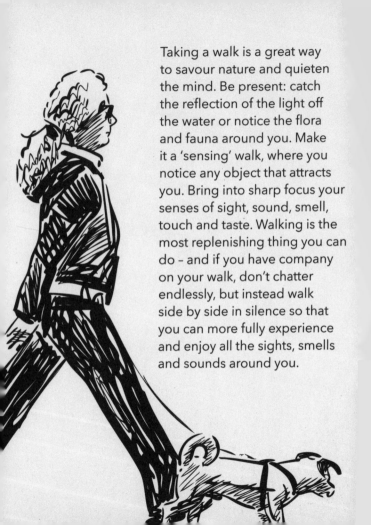

Taking a walk is a great way to savour nature and quieten the mind. Be present: catch the reflection of the light off the water or notice the flora and fauna around you. Make it a 'sensing' walk, where you notice any object that attracts you. Bring into sharp focus your senses of sight, sound, smell, touch and taste. Walking is the most replenishing thing you can do – and if you have company on your walk, don't chatter endlessly, but instead walk side by side in silence so that you can more fully experience and enjoy all the sights, smells and sounds around you.

Be
PASSIONATE
about
EVERYONE
and
EVERYTHING
that enters
your life.

Wayne Dyer

Try any kind of dance or movement class where you can enjoy the music and be aware of every fibre in your body as you move. It doesn't matter if you've got two left feet; nobody's watching you – just have fun!

If you are feeling uncomfortable about something, take slow, deep breaths and, if appropriate, bring your concerns to the relevant person. A helpful, mindful exercise to address any problem you are facing is to imagine you are close to the end of your life, and look back on the issue. Does it seem so important now?

We too should
make ourselves
empty, that the
great soul of the
universe may fill
us with its breath.

Laurence Binyon

Physical activity allows you to get more in touch with and more aware of your body. Mindful exercise is about performing physical activity while focusing inward. An increased flow of blood to the brain during exercise also allows you to be more open and aware. The idea is to let go of distractions and unrelated thoughts, and focus your attention on sensations, your breath, and the movements of your body.

Being mindful during your workout will significantly increase its effectiveness, decrease your chances of injury, enhance your enjoyment of exercising, and help you develop a healthy and loving relationship with your body. Remember, with mindful exercise you're going for quality, not quantity. Improve the efficacy of your workouts by turning off your TV or iPod and bringing your focused attention to your breath and your movements while you are jogging, cycling, swimming or lifting weights.

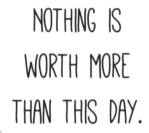

NOTHING IS
WORTH MORE
THAN THIS DAY.

Johann Wolfgang von Goethe

10am – Weekly Shop

1pm –

FREE TIME

3pm –
6pm – Cook Dinner

Plan to reduce the number of things on your 'to do' list for the day and set aside blocks of time without interruptions. Do less - do it more slowly, more fully and with more concentration.

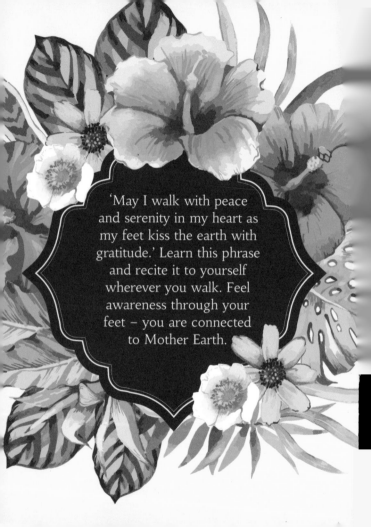

'May I walk with peace and serenity in my heart as my feet kiss the earth with gratitude.' Learn this phrase and recite it to yourself wherever you walk. Feel awareness through your feet – you are connected to Mother Earth.

LIKE CLOUDS IN THE SKY,
EVERYTHING IS IN A CONSTANT
PROCESS OF CHANGE.

The point of mindfulness is not to get rid of thought

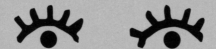

but to learn to see
thought skilfully.

Jack Kornfield

Why not try something for the first time? You are instinctively being mindful when your brain is engaged in something unfamiliar. If you experience a sensation of anxiety, fear, or resistance when facing a new activity, mindfully notice that you are experiencing fear of the unknown. Instead of shutting down or holding back, try something that you think of as less scary to begin with. Whether it's skydiving or a salsa class, by slowly building confidence you can enjoy new experiences and learn to embrace all that life has to offer.

Make a habit of looking out of your window at night, so that you can experience and appreciate those moments when the sky is full of stars, or have a full moon take your breath away.

Move outside
the outside
tangle
of
fear-thinking.

LIVE IN SILENCE.

Rumi

Our minds are full
of self-judgement,
providing a constant
noisy soundtrack in
our heads and often
holding us back in
life. Be aware of
this and notice how
it may be limiting
your decisions.

Allow
yourself to
let go of
stress and
perfectionism.

When you meditate, you allow thoughts to arise naturally. However, affirmations can help if you find you are stuck in a negative thought loop. Affirmations are quiet reminders that you repeat to yourself, either during your meditation or as you go about your day. Here are some examples of positive affirmations that may help:

I am the architect of my own life: I build its foundation and choose its contents.

Today, I am brimming with energy and overflowing with happiness.

Compassion washes away my anger and replaces it with love.

Happiness is a choice. I base my happiness on my own achievements and the blessings I've been given.

My ability to conquer my challenges is limitless: my potential to succeed is infinite.

Today, I abandon my old habits and take up new, more positive ones.

Everything that is happening now is happening for my ultimate good.

My fears of tomorrow are simply melting away.

I am at peace with all that has happened, is happening, and will happen.

Keep a notebook by your bed and record any dreams that you remember upon waking. Dreams are easily forgotten and this way you can catch them before they disappear. Sweet dreams!

Enjoy your sense of smell – rain-drenched earth, freshly baked bread, recently mown grass or barbeque smoke. Aromas help to move your awareness to the present moment.

Give yourself a mindfulness cue.
This could be the sound of a
pigeon cooing or a clock chiming
– something you will hear fairly
regularly, so that every time you
hear the sound you are reminded
to step back into a peaceful place.

Become aware of your habits
and how ingrained they are.
If you are stuck in a rut then
try shaking things up a little,
for example by drinking your
tea with lemon if you don't
normally, or taking a different
route to work in the morning.

Calm breath.
Calm mind.
Calm moment.

when walking,
walk.

when eating, eat.

Zen proverb

Hidden in the word

'listen'

is the word

'silent'.

Make silence a big part of your life, making a conscious effort to reduce your talking and switch off the noise around you, and see how silence can hold you in a calm space. Check in frequently to your inner silence as you go about your day.

For decision-making, you need to drop below the level of noise and chatter in your mind to the quiet, still space of your heart where you will hear your true voice – the one to listen to.

Reduce your information consumption. Cancel subscriptions for magazines you barely have time to read and unsubscribe from catalogues, junk mail and emails.

04

Learn to become conscious of your breath and visualise it filling the whole of your body. A few moments of this awareness will help you feel much lighter and brighter.

Hey There

You've been asleep
for a long time. zᶻᶻ

Isn't it time to awaken?

Ajahn Chah

Taking time to meditate is a big helping of mindfulness all in one go! Many people think that meditation should stop all our thoughts and rest our minds in thoughtless peace, but actually having thoughts while you meditate is perfectly normal. In fact, it's what's supposed to happen! Dealing with thoughts is how mindfulness meditation works. When you notice that you are distracted by your thoughts, gently bring your attention back to the object of your meditation, so that over time you will be able to relate differently to distractions, and increase your ability to focus and concentrate.

EMBRACE

THE PRESENT

MOMENT WITH

LOVE.

On waking, decide that you will look for the secret goodness in three people you deal with on a day-to-day basis. Open your heart as you speak with them during the day and notice how this intention affects things.

FEELINGS COME AND GO, LIKE CLOUDS IN A WINDY SKY. CONSCIOUS BREATHING IS MY ANCHOR.

Thích Nhất Hạnh

Good mindfulness practice
is to consider the concept
of non-attachment. It means
being flexible and not
clinging to a fixed idea.
Things don't always happen
the way you expect them
to. Learn to accept that.

Try something creative –
draw or *paint* a picture,
write a story about your
childhood or *play* a piece
of music. Don't worry
about the quality of what
you're producing, and
don't hold back – doing
it is the important part!

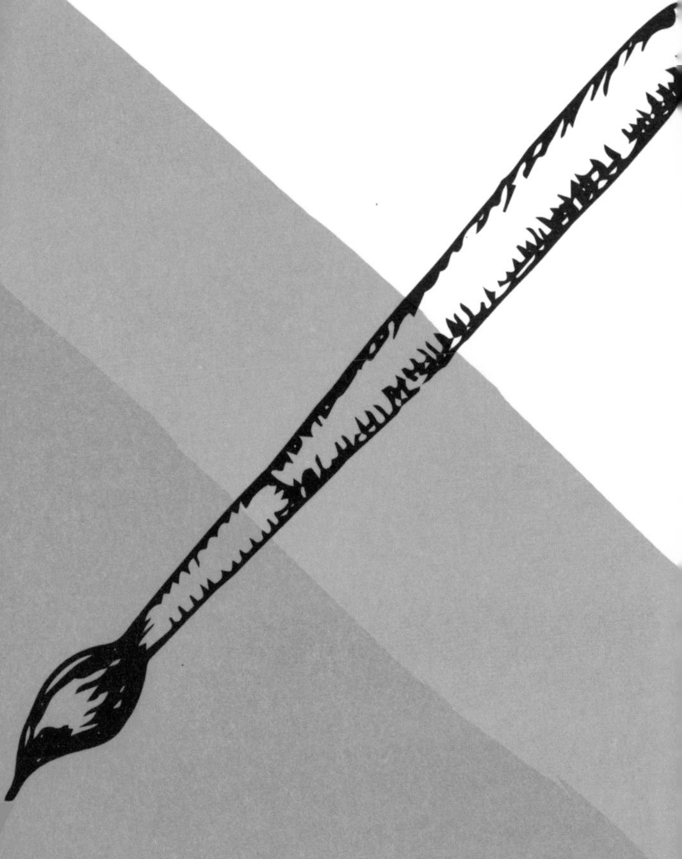

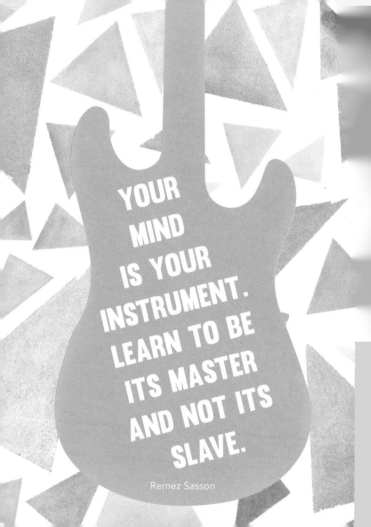

WE ARRIVE HERE WITH NOTHING AND WE LEAVE WITH NOTHING.

To distinguish between your work and your leisure, use your journey home to bring your mindful attention to your breath. Let go of the activities and worries of the working day and arrive home relaxed.

It may sound strange, but sometimes we forget to breathe! Deep breathing can be incredibly beneficial; try the following technique.

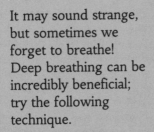

Place one hand over your chest

and one on your stomach.

Inhale through your nose with a closed mouth, then on the exhale, open your mouth and gently sigh. As you do, let your shoulders and the muscles of your upper body relax with the exhalation. Close your mouth and pause for a few seconds. Keep your mouth closed and inhale slowly through your nose and let your stomach rise up and out. When you've inhaled as much air as you can comfortably, stop. You're finished with that inhale.

Pause.

Open your mouth. Exhale through your mouth and gently pull your belly in.

Pause.

Do this two or three times, or as long as you need to feel steadier and more at ease.

Walking on water is certainly
miraculous, but walking peacefully on
earth is an even greater miracle.

John Gray

Light a candle and place it on the table before you eat. This brings calm and peace to a setting, alleviates tension, and encourages us to eat more slowly and thoughtfully. Take a moment to quietly give thanks for the food you are about to eat.

On waking in the morning, rather than springing out of bed to start your busy day, spend some moments becoming aware of your body, listening to the sounds around you and noticing what thoughts are in your mind.

Sit up and place your feet on the floor. Focus on your breathing and straighten your spine. As you breathe more deeply, allow your stomach to rise and fall. Notice how the space inside of you relaxes and your heart expands.

for fast-acting relief, try slowing down.

Lily Tomlin

When you look in the mirror, accept yourself with non-judgemental awareness and say, 'Thank you. This is who I am.' Understand and believe that everyone has beauty, and that includes you.

We are what we think.

All that we are
arises with our
thoughts.

With our thoughts,
we make our world.

Buddha

Never get so busy making a living that you forget to make a life. Travel if you can, no matter how near or far from home; it's the ultimate in mindful living.

When you're planning a journey or short trip, try not to just be eager to arrive at your destination: allow yourself to experience the new or surprising things along the way, and above all, enjoy every moment of it. When you return, it's great to have the memories, but don't start daydreaming about when your next trip away will be – be present in your daily life instead and enjoy the new perspective the time away has given you.

The ordinary can
be extraordinary.

If you have trouble remembering to incorporate mindfulness into your day, place little notes around home and work to act as prompts for you to

'breathe',
'remember'
and
'be mindful'.

Go for a walk in the rain, even if you don't feel like it! It adds another dimension to your surroundings and there can be a heightened sense of smell, sound and general awareness.

LET US NOT LOOK BACK IN ANGER OR FORWARD IN FEAR, BUT AROUND IN AWARENESS.

James Thurber

Having a wider heart and mind is more important than having a larger house.

Venerable Cheng Yen

The richness of the natural world is like food for our senses. Embrace your environment:

In *spring*, focus on the delicate perfume of a flower, or the scent of newly cut grass.

Choose a tree to observe over the days of *summer*, and enjoy its luscious greenery and majesty as it flourishes.

Experience nature in **autumn** by going out and walking amongst fallen leaves. Focus on their colour, their texture and the sound as you swoosh through them.

Early morning frosts and mist can transform the world around you in *winter*. Take a moment to admire the beauty that cold temperatures have created.

We can often be quick to jump to conclusions about people. When you next meet someone new, try to be aware of the judgements you automatically make. Reflect on your reactions, and think on ways you could nurture a less judgemental attitude in future.

Imagine the earth as seen from
outer space. Visualise this image
of the planet, and let your heart
send out love on a global scale,
rather than just to the people you
already know and care about.

SOMETIMES THE MOST IMPORTANT THING IN A WHOLE DAY IS THE REST WE TAKE BETWEEN TWO DEEP BREATHS.

Etty Hillesum

Everything you do can be done better from a place of relaxation.

Stephen C. Paul

Sometimes we get so caught up in being busy that we totally overlook our everyday posture. Several times a day, become aware of what posture you're in and how it feels within the body. If you closed your eyes, what would be the clues that you are standing, sitting, or lying down? For example if you are sitting in a chair with your eyes closed, what tells you that you are in a body that is sitting? Where do you feel pressure or movement? If you are slouching, gently straighten up.

At meals, sit on the front edge of your chair with your feet planted on the floor, knees a bit apart. Straighten the spine to maximise room for breathing. While sitting at your desk, become aware of your chair and how you are sitting. Ensure your feet are placed comfortably on the ground, and your back is straight with relaxed shoulders.

Whenever you're standing and waiting, perhaps in a queue, stand in a Mountain Pose with both feet firmly grounded, shoulders relaxed, back straight and pelvis tucked under. Breathe deeply and enjoy the wait!

Be especially
aware of your
judgements and
expectations and
let go of the stress
of perfectionism.
Accept things as
they happen and
accept people
for who they are,
including yourself.

Make time for your friends. Plan a day out or a picnic with a friend, and enjoy their company in a beautiful and relaxing location away from life's stresses. True friendships are about listening and speaking from the heart, so foster an open relationship between you where you can both share your thoughts and feelings. Take the time to really bond, and appreciate your special day together.

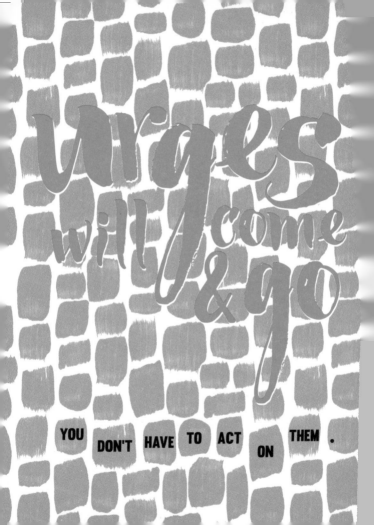

I took a deep
breath and listened
to the old brag of
my heart: I am,
I am, I am.

Sylvia Plath

Focus on an object
from nature such as
a flower or a seashell.
See its beauty and
intricacy, and place all
other thoughts to one
side while you marvel
at the detail of this
natural object.

REPEAT THESE WORDS AS FREQUENTLY AS YOU CAN:

'Let it be'

AND

'Calm abiding'.

NOTICE HOW IT ALLOWS YOU TO BE
ACCEPTING OF WHATEVER HAPPENS,
AND HELPS YOU TO MOVE PEACEFULLY
THROUGH YOUR DAY.

Let
us be
silent,

that we may
hear the
whispers of the
gods.

Ralph Waldo Emerson

Find five minutes (or more if you can spare it) every day in which to do absolutely nothing at all. Becoming comfortable with silence and stillness is essential to mindfulness practice. Whatever your state of mind or the number of things you have to do, rest for a moment between tasks and breathe for at least three complete breaths. This will give you a much needed energy recharge to carry on with your day.

Remember to allow yourself plenty of rest, especially when there are likely to be more demands on your time.

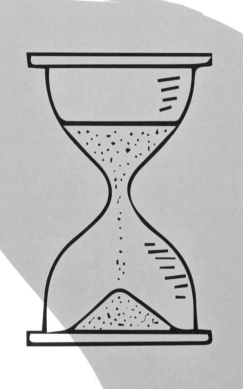

This moment is all there is.

Rumi

Before you go to bed,
spend a minute breathing
out the negative
experiences of the day,
breathing in serenity and
calm before you lie down
to sleep. Remind yourself
that all is well, and that
you are at peace.

WAITING
IS AN
OPPORTUNITY
FOR
MINDFULNESS.

We have **more** possibilities available in each **moment** than We realise.

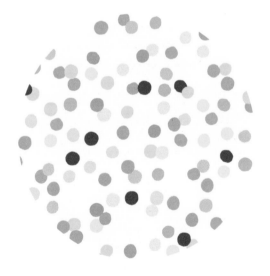

Thích Nhất Hạnh

Make your home your sanctuary, looking at ways you can make your environment as calm and peaceful as it can be. Decluttering or redecorating are both great ways to help let go of the past and renew your energy.

Place a bowl of water strewn with petals in your home to symbolically remind you to be at peace. Try placing wind chimes outside your window, and when you hear them chime let it remind you to take a deeper, slower breath towards peace and calm. Or you could create a display of objects that are meaningful; a candle and a picture of an inspirational person, perhaps. Sit by this space for a few quiet moments when you can.

Learn to
be

OK

with not

knowing.

If you are feeling overwhelmed, close your eyes and visualise ascending some steps. Take a step upwards with every breath, moving out of the dark confusion until you feel lighter at the top of the staircase.

If you want others to be **happy,** practise compassion.

If you want to be **happy,** practise compassion.

Dalai Lama

Before you go to sleep, lie perfectly still and send out loving thoughts to those close to you, those you work with, your community and the people of the world. It's important to also be a friend to yourself by expressing loving-kindness in all that you do. Even when you make mistakes, say this reminder, 'It's OK', and don't dwell on it if you haven't been as mindful as you would have liked during your day; there's always tomorrow to sharpen your senses!

Look for
the best in
everyone!

LIFE IS A CYCLE OF ENDINGS AND NEW BEGINNINGS.

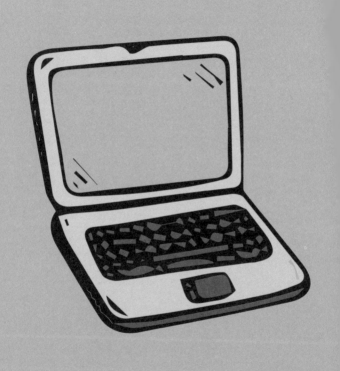

Have a digital detox for the day! This is especially effective at the weekend, or on any days off from work. Turn off your mobile, don't touch your computer, hide all gadgets and give yourself some time off from the endless technological invasion in your life. The non-stop stream of information we receive through these devices can be overwhelming, and it's good to give our mental 'inbox' a break from time to time.

If your mind won't slow down,
try observing and identifying your
emotions without having to resolve
them. 'I feel scared,' 'I feel worried,' 'I
feel angry,' etc. are all perfectly valid
emotions. Simply acknowledging
feelings is mindfulness in itself, and
can help you on a path to greater
clarity and peace.

FOR PEACE OF MIND WE
NEED TO RESIGN AS
GENERAL MANAGER OF
THE UNIVERSE.

Larry Eisenberg

It's amazing how the simple act of giving can have such a powerful effect on our well-being. Mahatma Gandhi once said, 'The best way to find yourself is to lose yourself in the service of others.' This couldn't be truer. It can be something simple like preparing a meal for friends or loved ones, organising a small surprise for someone special in your life that will make them happy or giving your time to someone in need. The benefit is that whatever you give, whether it's time, money, a gesture or a gift, you will almost certainly feel happier and richer for it.

When our minds are engulfed in worries, we are missing the experience of the moment.

There's never a day
when it's not good to
be thankful for the hot,
plentiful water that
provides your shower or
bath. It's worth reminding
yourself throughout
the day: 'Thank you.
I am truly blessed.'

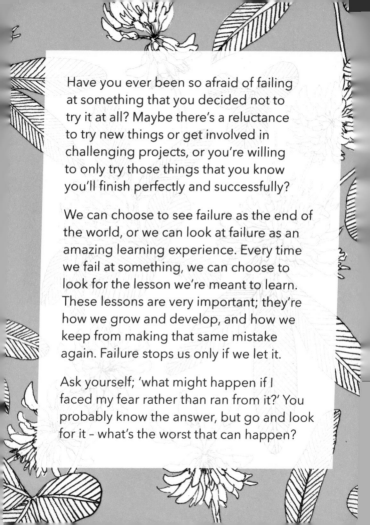

Have you ever been so afraid of failing at something that you decided not to try it at all? Maybe there's a reluctance to try new things or get involved in challenging projects, or you're willing to only try those things that you know you'll finish perfectly and successfully?

We can choose to see failure as the end of the world, or we can look at failure as an amazing learning experience. Every time we fail at something, we can choose to look for the lesson we're meant to learn. These lessons are very important; they're how we grow and develop, and how we keep from making that same mistake again. Failure stops us only if we let it.

Ask yourself; 'what might happen if I faced my fear rather than ran from it?' You probably know the answer, but go and look for it – what's the worst that can happen?

PEACE COMES FROM WITHIN.
DO NOT SEEK IT WITHOUT.

Buddha

IMAGINE THAT LIFE IS A MOVIE.
WATCH EVERYONE, INCLUDING
YOURSELF, AS THOUGH YOU
ARE THE AUDIENCE. RELAX
AND SEE HOW LIFE FLOWS
BEFORE YOU. DON'T GET
CAUGHT UP IN THE DRAMA.

COME HOME TO THE PRESENT

Help reduce the potential for stress and anxiety in your life by planning. If you are constantly rushing to appointments and other commitments, try giving yourself a more realistic timeframe. You'll arrive less stressed and more fully present.

When you have big decisions to make, sitting in stillness and meditating on your breath offers you the space to tap into your inner wisdom. With practice you will learn to trust your own intuition and discover steady answers to your life's requests.

THE ABILITY
TO SIMPLIFY
MEANS TO
ELIMINATE THE
UNNECESSARY
SO THAT THE
NECESSARY
MAY SPEAK.

Hans Hofmann

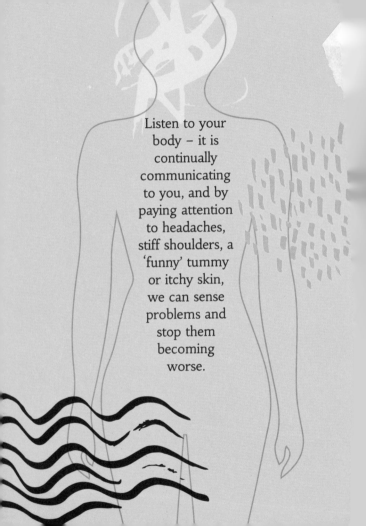

Listen to your body – it is continually communicating to you, and by paying attention to headaches, stiff shoulders, a 'funny' tummy or itchy skin, we can sense problems and stop them becoming worse.

Carry lavender oil with
you so that you can
refresh yourself and your
space wherever you are.
The oil can be rubbed
on to pulse points to aid
relaxation and create a
sense of calm.

ANXIETY DOES NOT *EMPTY* **EMPTY** *tomorrow* **OF ITS** *sorrows,*

BUT

ONLY EMPTIES

today

OF ITS

strength.

IS A JOURNEY, NOT A DESTINATION.

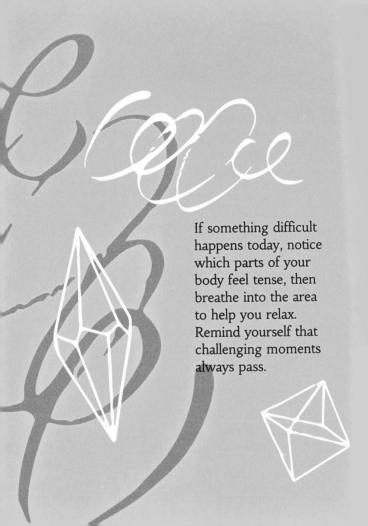

If something difficult happens today, notice which parts of your body feel tense, then breathe into the area to help you relax. Remind yourself that challenging moments always pass.

Every breath is an opportunity
to receive and let go.

I receive love
and I let go of
pain.

Brenda MacIntyre

Try to take the 'chore' out of doing the housework. Focus on what you are physically doing rather than rushing through it. View it as a positive and loving commitment to your home, completed with thorough care.

Listening to music can be a great mindfulness exercise. Choose music that is soothing: instrumental or classical are good choices. Begin by setting yourself up in a comfortable and upright posture. Choose a space where you can minimise any outer distractions and be sure to remove any background electronic disturbances such as phones, computers or the television. Spend a few moments resting your attention on the breath, breathing fully and completely and really immersing yourself when you inhale and exhale.

As you begin to listen to the music, focus with intention on the sound and vibration of each note, the feelings that the music brings up within you and other sensations that are happening 'right now' as you listen.

If other thoughts creep into your head, gently bring your attention back to the current moment and the music you are hearing. Afterwards, notice how much calmer you feel.

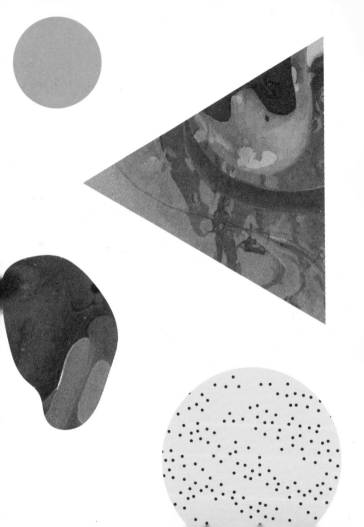